MW00616030

quaking marsh

Stuart Bartow

quaking marsh

copyright © 2017 Stuart Bartow
ISBN 978-1-947271-05-0

Pond Frog Editions
A division of
Red Moon Press
PO Box 2461
Winchester VA
22604-1661 USA
www.redmoonpress.com

first printing

The author thanks the editors of the following publications where some of these haiku first appeared: *Acorn: A Journal of Contemporary Haiku; Akitsu Quarterly; a hundred gourds; Haiku Society of America Members' Anthology 2016; The Heron's Nest; Modern Haiku; New England Letters; Shamrock: Journal of the Irish Haiku Society; Wild Plum; Write Like Issa: a haiku how-to.*

POND FROG
EDITIONS

For Barbara

quaking marsh

quaking marsh
how she stirs
in her sleep

for an instant
forgetting where
in the stars

light rainfall last night
briefly
her footsteps

the spider's sign language

the thread
between us

repairing the halo
around the street light
a flurry of moths

spring traffic jam
all of us stuck
in a dandelion storm

country road
         my truck dodging
love- crazed sparrows

don't believe
in the hermit thrush
the forest sings

new neighbors next door — starlings

quaking marsh
beneath the black water
heartbeats

the little girl
her hand out the car window
catches me

hearing the wind chimes

without the wind

waking before dawn
to hear the train
extinct for decades idle?

spring sermon
mind keeps wandering
to those legs

the lost boy briefly
in the wood
thrush's song

each night
creating cities
to wander in

beyond the radio's static
songs
sailing the stars

midnight moth
the moons of Jupiter
mapped on her wings

fireflies briefly Ursa Major

green comet dream's return at 5 a.m.

all their wings together
make the same song
bumblebees

ladybird lights
on the open book of poems
alphabets of stars

the marsh in midsummer bullfrogs translating

fastening my porch to the sky spiders

summer symphony
between movements
katydids

my cat out stalking
grasshoppers
be still

stowaway in my kayak
where's home
wolf spider

casting into its reflection
what kind of fish
live under the moon

windy day
the scarecrow directing
crow traffic

windless night
still the branches
swaying

meteor shower
stars still falling
even in daylight

a thousand crickets auditioning for the moon

huddled undertakers
in the rain
turkey vultures

autumn wind

we hold each other closer

power outage
the stars
waiting

starlight or hoarfrost
which magic   to believe

another birthday
the scarecrow and I
grow more alike

orb weavers
doing the world's work
on the graveyard shift

abandoned bee hive
as though the tree's soul
has fled

only crows visit
the cemetery
of tilting stones

the scarecrow wears it better
my old
plaid shirt

tall weeds
one or two crickets
still calling

cold night
the cats keep pestering me
to go to bed

first winter storm
the feral tom
moves in

feeding the woodstove
the house creaks
sailing through winter

winter morning
chickadees and the wind
do all the talking

fox tracks in the snow
disappearing
act

I too would choose these woods chickadees

summer's bees
frozen
into winter stars

below zero
even the scarecrow
looks cold

February thaw
go back to sleep
ladybirds

the marsh awakens
from its dream of winter
spring peepers

STUART BARTOW teaches writing and literature a SUNY (State University of New York) Adirondack. He is chair of the Battenkill Conservancy, an environmental group working at the New York-Vermont border. His prose work, *Teaching Trout to Talk: the Zen of Small Stream Fly Fishing*, received the 2014 best book of non-fiction award from the Adirondack Center for Writing. He has previously published six books of poetry. This is his first book of haiku.